SCIENCE MISSIONS

Cloning
Pets

Sean Stewart Price

EXPRESS EDITION

Chicago, Illinois

www.heinemannraintree.com
Visit our website to find out more information about Heinemann-Raintree books.

To order:

☎ Phone 888-454-2279

🖳 Visit www.heinemannraintree.com to browse our catalog and order online.

Edited by Adam Miller, Andrew Farrow, and Adrian Vigliano
Designed by Philippa Jenkins
Original illustrations © Capstone Global Library Ltd.
Illustrated by KJA-artists.com
Picture research by Tracy Cummins
Production by Alison Parsons
Originated by Capstone Global Library Ltd
Printed in the United States of America by Worzalla Publishing

14 13 12 11 10
10 9 8 7 6 5 4 3 2 1

Library of Congress Cataloging-in-Publication Data
Cataloging-in-Publication data is on file at the Library of Congress.

ISBN: 978-1-4109-3991-3 (HC)
978-1-4109-3998-2 (PB)

Acknowledgments
The author and publishers are grateful to the following for permission to reproduce copyright material: AP Photo/John Chadwick **p. 9**; Corbis ©EPA/GARY I ROTHSTEIN **pp. 4 & 5**; Corbis ©Lester V. Bergman **p. 6**; Corbis ©Najlah Feanny **p. 8**; Corbis ©Jim Richardson **p. 17**; Corbis ©GARY I ROTHSTEIN/epa **p. 20**; Corbis ©zhou qi/XinHua/Xinhua Press **p. 23**; Corbis ©Reuters **p. 26**; Corbis ©JO YONG-HAK/Reuters **p. 34**; Corbis ©Stewart Cohen **p. 38**; Corbis ©Sanford/ Agliolo **p. 39**; Corbis ©RBM Online/Handout/ Reuters **p. 43**; Corbis ©Steve & Ann Toon/Robert Harding World Imagery **p. 47**; FLPA ©Hugh Clark **p. 45**; Getty Images/GABRIEL BOUYS/AFP **p. 22**; Getty Images/Texas A&M University **p. 27**; Getty Images/Peter Sherrard **pp. 32 & 33**; Getty Images/Steve Gorton and Tim Ridley **p. 35**; Getty Images/Paul Nicklen **p. 36**; Getty Images/Erik Sampers **p. 37**; Getty Images/Chip Somodevilla **p. 48**; istockphoto ©Dan Brandenburg **p. 21**; istockphoto ©paul kline **pp. 18 & 19**; Mary Evans/ITC/LEW GRADE/PRODUCERS CIRCLE/Ronald Grant Archive **p. 42**; Photo Researchers, Inc./Russell Kightley **pp. 10 & 11**; Photo Researchers, Inc./ BSIP **p. 13**; Photo Researchers, Inc./Professor Miodrag Stojkovic **p. 15**; Photo Researchers, Inc./Gusto **p. 28**; Photo Researchers, Inc./ Hybrid Medical **p. 29**; Photo Researchers, Inc./ Philippe Psaila **p. 30**; Photo Researchers **p. 44**; Photo Researchers, Inc./Mark Newman **p. 46**; Shutterstock ©Gilles DeCruyenaere **p. 7**; Shutterstock ©Andresr **p. 12**; Shutterstock ©HomeStudio **pp. 50 & 51**; THE KOBAL COLLECTION/LUCASFILM/20TH CENTURY FOX **pp. 24 & 25**; THE KOBAL COLLECTION/MBLIN/ UNIVERSAL **pp. 40 & 41**.

Cover photograph of cloned beagles reproduced with the permission of Getty Images.

We would like to thank Ann Fullick for her invaluable help in the preparation of this book.

Every effort has been made to contact copyright holders of any material reproduced in this book. Any omissions will be rectified in subsequent printings if notice is given to the publisher.

CONTENTS

Some words are printed in bold, **like this**. You can find out what they mean by looking in the glossary. You can also look out for them in the **WORD STORE** box at the bottom of each page.

SEND IN THE
CLONES

This Labrador retriever cost his owners $155,000. Why?

Because he is a **clone**. A clone is an exact copy of another living thing. It has the same **genes** as the original. Genes are the instructions for life. They are found within **cells** (the tiny building blocks of life). Genes decide if something grows into a gerbil or a person. They decide how a living thing will look, grow, and more.

The dog's owners had loved another Labrador retriever. His name was Sir Lancelot. After Sir Lancelot died, a company used his cells to make Sir Lancelot Encore, the clone. But cloning is very complicated. It takes a long time. That is why it is so expensive.

Sir Lancelot Encore is one of the first cloned dogs in the United States. Will there be more like him? The price of pet cloning is going down. But it is still not clear if people will want to clone their pets. And if they do, what will that mean for other pets? What will it mean for other animals? And what will it mean for people?

This shows Sir Lancelot
Encore at 10 weeks old.

How common is cloning?

To many people, making copies of living things, or **cloning**, sounds like an idea from the future. Yet humans have been cloning plants for thousands of years.

Making an exact copy, or clone, of a plant is fairly easy. Farmers can take a twig or cutting from one plant. Then they attach it to another. Sometimes, if they put the twig in water, it will grow. It will have the same **genes** (instructions for life) as the first plant. Many common plants are grown this way, including Red Delicious apples.

In nature, simple animals can also clone themselves. You can cut planarian worms into three pieces. Each piece will grow into a separate worm. Each worm will be a clone of the original. (Don't try this on other worms. It is cruel and will not work.)

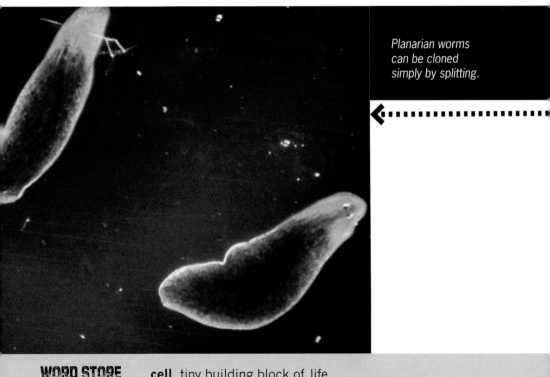

Planarian worms can be cloned simply by splitting.

WORD STORE   **cell** tiny building block of life
clone act of making a copy; also, the copy itself

How to clone a frog

Just about anyone can clone plants or simple animals. But cloning complex animals requires scientific knowledge. From the 1950s to the 1970s, a series of experiments led to cloned frogs. How was the cloning done?:

Cloning more complicated animals, like this leopard frog, is a difficult process.

1. Scientists used a thin glass tube to suck the center from a frog egg **cell**. This part of the cell is called the **nucleus**. The nucleus is the control center of a cell. It tells it how to grow.

2. Then they took the nucleus from another frog egg cell. They put this nucleus into the frog egg cell missing its nucleus.

3. Then this new egg cell was put inside a female frog. Scientists waited to see if a baby frog could be grown this way.

Embryo cells

These frog experiments worked. A baby frog eventually grew. As a result, scientists knew that frog egg cells could be cloned. These cells are called **embryo** cells. An embryo is an animal in an early step of growth. But could the cells of adult animals be cloned?

This photo shows Dolly the cloned sheep.

Dolly's world

July 5, 1996, was an important day for **cloning**. In a shed near Roslin, Scotland, a group of scientists watched a lamb being born. But this was no ordinary animal.

Dolly, the lamb, was a clone. To clone Dolly, scientists used a **cell** taken from an adult Finn Dorset sheep. (See page 16 for more on this process.) Creating Dolly proved difficult. It took 276 failed attempts before she was born.

Dolly lived for six years. This is about half the life span of a normal sheep. She died of a lung disease that usually strikes much older sheep. Dolly was badly overweight. She also had other health problems.

WORD STORE   **mammal** animal that gives milk to its young and usually has hair or fur

These health issues might have been because she was a clone. Or they might have been caused by something else. Nobody is sure. But during her life, Dolly gave birth to several of her own healthy lambs. That proved that clones could **reproduce** (have young) normally.

Scottish scientists Keith Campbell (middle) and Ian Wilmut (right) stand with Dolly, the clone they created. Also pictured is Dr. Ron James (left). He was the director of an organization that helped the scientists with their work.

Join the club

Since Dolly's birth, scientists have cloned many more animals. They include mice, rats, rabbits, goats, pigs, cattle, mules, horses, cats, and dogs. But each success took place after many failures.

Dolly changed the way people look at cloning. Suddenly, scientists could clone a large **mammal**. A mammal is an animal that gives milk to its young and usually has hair or fur. Cloning large living things like cows and even humans no longer seemed impossible.

HOW TO MAKE A
CLONE

Cells are life's building blocks. People, dogs, and sheep are made up of trillions of cells. Each cell is alive. It grows, gathers fuel, **reproduces** (makes copies), and dies.

And each cell contains a blueprint, or set of instructions. That blueprint decides whether something will be a person, a dog, or a sheep. It also helps decide how something will grow. For example, it decides the color of a person's skin or the length of a person's arm bones.

A cell's **nucleus** is its control center. The nucleus of just one cell contains all the information needed to make a copy of a living thing. That information is used to make a **clone**.

In some ways, cloning is very easy to understand. But cloning is extremely hard to do. Scientists fail at it far more often than they succeed.

This diagram shows a cell cut in half. This helps to show how complex a single cell is!

nucleus

Natural-born clones

Can animals produce **clones** naturally? Yes. Some twins are natural clones.

Identical twins come from one egg. They are created when an **embryo** splits at an early step of growth (see the diagram at right). This creates two of the exact same embryo. Identical twins have identical **genes**. They are the same sex and look alike. They are natural clones.

Fraternal twins come from two eggs. They are different embryos. They have different genes. They can be the same sex, or one can be a boy and the other a girl. They do not always look alike. They are not clones.

Natural twins are born to humans as well as animals. These twins are identical.

Natural twins are common in the animal kingdom. They can be found among cats, sheep, ferrets, deer, cattle, armadillos, and other animals. So, creating clones of animals is not unusual in nature.

But the clones made in laboratories are **artificial** clones. They are made by people, not by nature. These clones are in many ways just like twins. But they also offer scientists new possibilities for research (see pages 14 and 15).

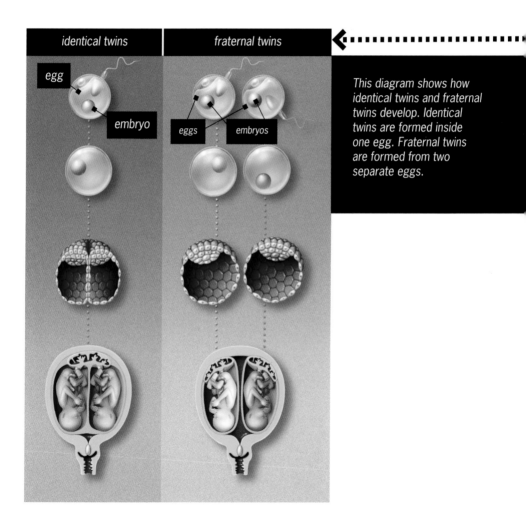

identical twins

fraternal twins

egg

embryo

eggs

embryos

This diagram shows how identical twins and fraternal twins develop. Identical twins are formed inside one egg. Fraternal twins are formed from two separate eggs.

Artificial cloning

There are three different kinds of **artificial cloning**.

Reproductive cloning

The best-known type of artificial cloning is **reproductive cloning**. This is the type of cloning that gave us Encore and Dolly. This technology creates an animal that has the same **DNA** as another animal. DNA carries the blueprint, or instructions, for how a body is made up (see the box below).

WHAT IS DNA?

WHAT IS DNA?
DNA is short for "deoxyribonucleic acid." DNA is found in the center of the cell, the **nucleus**. It is like a blueprint for life. Sections of DNA carry specific instructions for how a body will be made up. For example, they give instructions for white fur on a dog. These sections of DNA are genes.

Therapeutic cloning

Another type of artificial cloning is called **therapeutic cloning**. It is the cloning of human **embryos** for research. Embryos are animals in an early step of growth. The goal is not to create cloned human beings. Instead, this kind of cloning is used to make a special kind of **cell**. It is called a **stem cell**.

Stem cells can be used to create any type of cell in the human body. Researchers hope that stem cells could be used to create replacement cells. These could treat heart disease, cancer, and other health problems.

WORD STORE   **reproductive cloning** scientific process that creates an animal with the same DNA, or set of instructions, as another animal

This is a close-up view of human stem cells.

Gene cloning

Gene cloning is another kind of artificial cloning. Scientists copy individual **genes**. These genes can then be added to the DNA coding of another plant or animal. This process is called **genetic engineering**. Genetic engineering is used to study different diseases (see page 23).

How to clone a cat

So, how would scientists **clone** an animal? They must follow a process with many steps. The following steps show the process of **reproductive cloning** for a cat:

1. First, you need two cats. The first cat will have its **cells** cloned. The other cat must be an adult female. She will provide an egg cell. This cell must not have started to develop into a new cat yet.

2. Take the cells of the cat to be cloned. For example, take skin cells. Then, take the egg from the adult female cat. Remove the **nucleus** from that egg. (Remember: The nucleus contains the basic instructions, or **DNA**, of how to make the cat.)

3. Place the skin cell next to the egg cell missing its nucleus. Zap them with electricity. If everything goes right, this will cause the skin cell to join with the empty egg cell. Together they form a new cell.

4. If it works, this process will create an early-stage **embryo**. The embryo is put into another female cat. The cat that carries this embryo is called the **surrogate** mother (see the box on page 17).

5. The clone embryo grows inside the surrogate mother. The clone is then born as a kitten. But it contains the same DNA as the first cat (the cat to be cloned).

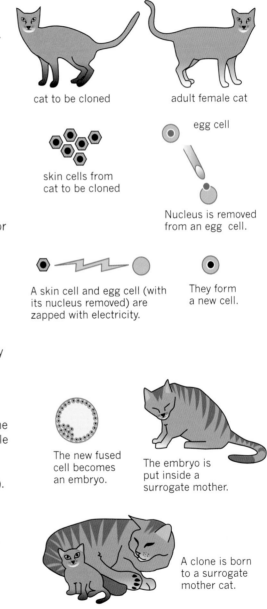

cat to be cloned

adult female cat

egg cell

skin cells from cat to be cloned

Nucleus is removed from an egg cell.

A skin cell and egg cell (with its nucleus removed) are zapped with electricity.

They form a new cell.

The new fused cell becomes an embryo.

The embryo is put inside a surrogate mother.

A clone is born to a surrogate mother cat.

SURROGATE MOTHERS

Surrogate means "substitute." A clone's mother is a surrogate mother. She carries the baby and gives birth to it. But the clone baby carries none of this mother's DNA. Instead the DNA comes from the animal that provided the cells.

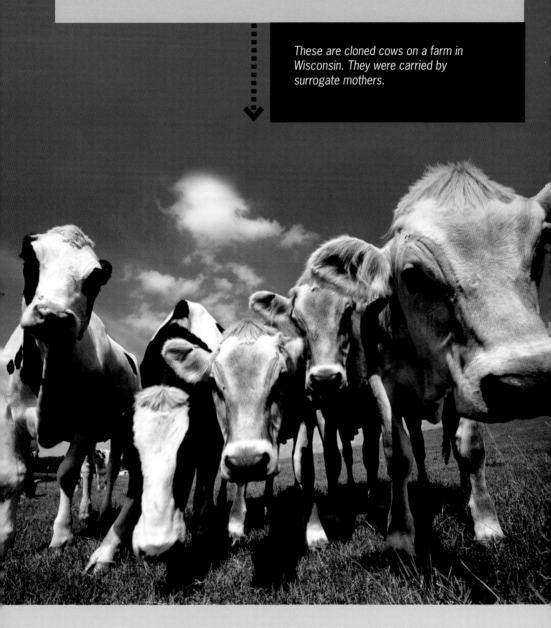

These are cloned cows on a farm in Wisconsin. They were carried by surrogate mothers.

WHY
CLONE?

Why would someone **clone** an animal? Why go through all the trouble? Why spend all the money?

One reason is that humans love their pets. In 2008 there were an estimated 82 million cats and 72 million dogs in the United States. People also have millions of fish, gerbils, hamsters, mice, and other small creatures.

Another reason is that people make money by selling pets and farm animals. These people often produce and train special kinds of dogs. Dogs that are expert trackers bring a high price. The same is true of cows that produce a lot of meat. Cloning might be expensive right now. But as it becomes cheaper to do, it could help people make a lot of money.

Many people form a special bond with their pets.

For the love of an animal

Edgar and Nina Otto had Sir Lancelot Encore **cloned** in 2009. The Ottos had loved Sir Lancelot, their original Labrador retriever. When he became ill in 2003, they had scientists take a small amount of **cells** from him. These cells contained Sir Lancelot's **DNA**. This had the instructions they would need for a clone. They had the cells frozen.

The Ottos pose with Sir Lancelot Encore. Nina Otto shows a picture of Sir Lancelot.

Most animal-rights groups are against cloning. These groups work to make sure animals are treated well. They have two main problems with cloning:

1. The cloning process can be dangerous for the animals involved (see page 30).

2. There are many pets in animal shelters that need homes.

Critics argue that people should adopt pets, not clone them.

The Ottos were encouraged when the first cloned dog, Snuppy, was born in the country of South Korea in 2005. They would not mind paying $155,000 to clone Sir Lancelot.

Some people said the Ottos wasted their money. Critics said that their money could have helped thousands of already-living pets in animal shelters. The Humane Society of the United States and the Royal Society for the Prevention of Cruelty to Animals in the United Kingdom are both against the practice of pet cloning. (See the box above.)

But the Ottos did not want just any dog. They wanted a copy of Sir Lancelot. "He was a wonderful dog," said Nina Otto. "Money wasn't an object. We just wanted our wonderful, loving dog back."

Cloning for money

For centuries, humans have **bred** animals to make them more useful. Breeding means controlling how animals create their young. For example, fast horses have been bred with other fast horses to make even faster horses. Pigs have been bred to have the most meat. Dogs have been bred for their sense of smell. Many people believe that **cloning** is another way for people to breed animals.

Selective cloning

Many supporters believe that this is the strongest argument for animal cloning. Breeders could select their best animals to be cloned. Once cloned, these animals could be bred with others. They could produce even better animals. Cloning would just be one more helpful tool for animal breeders.

These are clones of a dog named Trakr. Trakr was a great sniffing dog. He helped the rescue operation after the September 11, 2001, terrorist attacks.

WORD STORE   **breed** control how animals mate and reproduce

Many people confuse cloning with **genetic engineering**. Cloning is when you make an exact copy of a living thing. The **DNA** is exactly the same. But genetic engineering is different. In genetic engineering, scientists only change individual **genes** within the DNA coding of a plant or animal. For instance, mice can be genetically engineered to carry disease-causing genes. Scientists can then study these mice to learn more about how certain diseases are passed on within human families. They can also study how to cure these diseases.

WHAT COULD GO
WRONG?

In early 2009, a company called BioArts International seemed ready to make money from pet **cloning**. BioArts had produced the clone of Sir Lancelot. It expected many more orders for cloned dogs.

Then something strange happened. BioArts offered a "Golden Clone Giveaway." The winner could have his or her dog cloned for free. Newspapers and television stations covered this story widely. BioArts expected tens of thousands of people to enter. But just 237 people signed up for the giveaway. This clearly meant that there was little demand for dog cloning.

Lack of demand is one big reason that BioArts stopped cloning dogs in 2009. But there are other reasons as well. Some of those reasons have to do with flaws in the process. Others are because cloning does not always produce expected results.

Some movies and books about the future present scenes like this army of identical, robotic clones. These are not the results cloning will likely lead to!

A second chance?

A **clone** is an exact **genetic** copy of the original dog, cat, or other creature. This means it has the same **DNA**. But this does not mean the clone will look and act exactly like the original. Clones often act and look differently than expected.

For example, a Brahman bull named Chance won many competitions. He was very calm. When Chance died in 1998, scientists offered to clone this rare kind of bull.

The result was a bull named Second Chance. He looked just like Chance. But Second Chance was much more aggressive. The new bull stabbed his owner twice with his horns.

This shows that DNA is not the only thing that affects behavior. An animal's experiences and surroundings also play a big role in how it behaves.

This photo shows Second Chance and his owner.

WORD STORE genetic relating to genes

Switching on the right genes

Sometimes the cloned animal does not even look like the original. Take the case of CC. In 2001 CC became the world's first cloned cat. (The initials CC stand for "Copy Cat.") But CC did not look like Rainbow, the original cat. Rainbow had black, orange, and white fur. But CC had no orange fur.

As it turns out, one **cell** can have different **genes** for fur color. Some of these genes are switched on and others are switched off. CC had different genes switched on than Rainbow. So, she looked different.

Cloning and health

Most **cloned** animals are born healthy and stay that way. They are able to have young and live normal lives.

But some clones suffer from odd health problems. For instance, as discussed earlier, Dolly the sheep clone died at age six. That is about half the normal life span for a sheep (see the box at right). Second Chance, the Brahman bull, died at age eight. That was less than half the life span of Chance, the original bull. These health issues might have had nothing to do with cloning. But scientists are not sure.

Dolly the sheep is now stuffed. She is on display in a museum in Scotland.

WORD STORE   immune system body system that helps fight disease

About 25 percent of clones are born with health issues that the original animal did not have. Many cloned animals start life with enlarged organs (such as the heart and liver). This creates serious health problems. Others have problems with their **immune systems**. This is the body system that helps fight disease. Some develop problems with their bones and joints (areas where bones meet). Obesity, or being very overweight, seems to be a common problem.

CELL "CLOCKS"

Some health problems might be tied to the kind of **cells** used in cloning. Cells from adult animals are often used in cloning. Each of these cells has a kind of clock. It is made of something called **telomeres** (pictured below). Telomeres are pieces of **DNA**. This telomere clock in adult cells is far ahead of the clock in cells in an earlier step of development (**embryos**).

This does not mean that clones are born at the same age as the animal the cells came from. The clones are born as babies, just like any other animal. But it does mean that some animals cloned from adult cells might have a shorter life span than other animals.

Cloning is hard on animals

Many people believe **cloning** hurts animals. For instance, the birth of Dolly came only after 276 failed attempts. This is a lot of testing for animals to go through. In 2003 scientists tried 716 times to clone rhesus monkeys. Every effort failed. So far, scientists still have not been able to create a **primate** clone. Primates are a group of animals that includes monkeys, apes, and humans.

It currently takes at least 12 dogs in order to produce 1 cloned puppy. The dogs either provide the **genetic** material (**DNA**) or the egg. Some act as a **surrogate** mother, meaning they carry and give birth to the puppy. The process of cloning can be stressful for animals. Cloning companies won't say how many animals die in the process. Yet people who study cloning say that it is becoming safer all the time.

A scientist uses a mouth-operated tube to move cells.

WORD STORE   **primate** group of animals that includes monkeys, apes, and humans

The way **cells** are shipped before the cloning process is important. Many cells are simply shipped while frozen in ice. Others are shipped in more controlled containers. They keep the temperature steady. The cells frozen in ice often show unusual growth. Those shipped in more controlled containers are usually fine.

Freezing cells in ice may harm them.

MYTHS ABOUT CLONES

Throughout history, some people have feared twins. Ancient stories from Greece and Rome told of twins or look-alikes who were tricksters, or people to be feared. Ancient Aztec people saw twins as a threat to their parents. Very often, one of the twins would be killed at birth.

Today, twins are less likely to create such worry. But the trickster image still lives on. It can be seen in characters like the Weasley twins in the *Harry Potter* series. Twins often seem to be portrayed as up to mischief.

This long-held suspicion about twins partly explains why **clones** make people uneasy. Clones are basically twins made by science. So, people fear not only the twins. They also fear that nature is being changed in ways that it should not be.

Perhaps that is why there are so many **myths** (ideas not based on fact) about cloning. And perhaps that is why cloning remains unpopular with many people.

Some people fear a future in which cloning makes everyone the same. This fear is based mostly on myths.

We will look at some of the most popular myths about clones. First, some people believe the myth that a clone will have the same memories as the original animal. But this is not true.

Individuals

A clone is a **genetic** copy of an animal. But clones are individual animals. A clone grows up with completely different experiences than the original animal. The clone can also grow up in a completely different place than the original. So, it will have completely different memories.

This can get confusing, because **genes** *can* affect animal's behavior. A clone might react to certain events in the same way as the original. It might have a similar personality. For instance, the owners of the bull Second Chance noticed that it behaved a lot like Chance, the original bull. The two animals ate and slept exactly the same way.

Cloned animals
have different
experiences
and memories
than the original
animal.

Clones give birth to normal babies, not clones.

But Second Chance turned into a much different animal. Chance was gentle enough to be around people. But Second Chance became aggressive easily. This shows that a clone is an individual.

Along these same lines, some people believe the **offspring** (babies) of clones are clones themselves. This is also not true. Cloned animals can **reproduce** just like any other animals. Their offspring are not clones. They are ordinary baby animals. They are individuals.

WORD STORE   **offspring** young (babies)

Many people think that **clones** are unnatural creatures. They think people should fear them. This is another **myth**.

People who think this way believe cloning is a new process. They feel that we do not know what to expect from it. But we have been eating cloned food for centuries.

For example, a banana takes about 30 years to grow from seed. So, farmers speed the process along. To do this, they clone bananas. Starfish and many other simple animals also make copies of themselves by cloning.

So, cloning can be a very natural process. However, **mammals** and other complex animals have only recently been cloned by scientists.

Starfish can clone themselves naturally.

Many people who fear cloning also confuse plant cloning with animal cloning. They believe that a cloned animal's **DNA** has somehow been inserted into another live animal. They fear that cloning is the ability to change one type of live animal into another. This is simply not true. Scientists are not using cloning to create strange new creatures.

Bananas are an example of a food that has been cloned by humans.

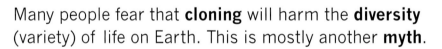

Many people worry how diseases will affect cloned animals.

Many people fear that **cloning** will harm the **diversity** (variety) of life on Earth. This is mostly another **myth**.

In nature, animals have young when a mother and father come together. The couple produces children. Each child gets a mix of **genes** from both parents. This results in endless combinations of genes. It creates great diversity. Each child will have a unique combination of his or her parents' genes.

Diversity helps all **species** survive. (A species is a group of animals that is created in nature.) For instance, a disease might hit many members of a species. But if the species is diverse, some individuals will have protection against that disease in their genes. As a result, the species will survive.

WORD STORE   **diversity** variety
species group of similar animals that is created in nature

But if that same disease hit a group of clones, the story might be different. They all have the same exact same mix of genes. What if the clones had no protection against the disease? Most or all of the species could be wiped out.

Does this mean pet cloning is dangerous? Probably not. Pet cloning remains expensive. As a result, there are very few cloned animals. And the cloned animals that are out there are very different from one another. So, cloning will not hurt diversity among animals. They are also not enough cloned farm animals to cause worry.

However, cloning could become a problem in farming. For example, many scientists currently worry about cloned plant crops. These crops are all the same. Scientists worry that whole crops could be wiped out by disease. The crops do not have enough diversity.

Some people worry that cloned farm animals will lead to diversity problems.

EXTREME CLONING

Books and movies often affect people's opinions. When it comes to **cloning**, they have had a huge impact. Almost always, books and movies show cloning as something to be feared.

One of the best-known books to deal with cloning is Aldous Huxley's *Brave New World* (1932). In it, Huxley presented a scary future world in which humans are created by cloning. Likewise, the movie *Jurassic Park* (1993) turned animal cloning into a nightmare. In the movie, a scientist manages to bring back dinosaurs. Dinosaurs are **extinct** (have died out). Yet he **reproduces** the dinosaurs by cloning. At first, this seems like a great idea. But the dinosaurs get out of control and terrorize people.

Many other books and movies play on fears about cloning. For instance, the *Star Wars* movies show clones as mindless soldiers working for an evil emperor. Some of these problems are unlikely to ever happen. But they affect people's opinions when they talk about cloning.

A cloned dinosaur is hatched by a scientist in the movie Jurassic Park.

Cloning humans

First in the 1970s, and then in the 2000s, scientists claimed to have **cloned** humans. In both cases, the claims made people very nervous. People feared that human clones would soon become a reality. But in both cases, the claims proved false.

Some people argue that fears about human cloning are overblown. They also point out that human cloning could have positive effects. For instance, some people carry illnesses in their **genes**. Cloning could allow a couple to not pass on specific disease-causing genes to their children.

This movie from 1978 was about an evil plan to create dozens of clones of German World War II leader Adolf Hitler!

Opponents of cloning

However, others believe that human **reproductive cloning** (what created Dolly and Encore) is wrong. They also fear that cloning could be combined with **genetic engineering**. As we have seen (see page 23), genetic engineering involves changing an animal's genes. This could lead to "designer human beings," meaning people designed to have specific, good features. This might weaken the **genetic diversity** of humans. If all humans had the same genes, they all might be wiped out by the same disease.

*This is a cloned human **embryo**. Scientists have made major steps toward cloning humans. But a human clone has not been born yet.*

Could cloning bring back extinct species?

The movie *Jurassic Park* was based on a 1990 best-selling book by Michael Crichton. In the book, a scientist develops an amusement park that features live dinosaurs.

In the story, the dinosaurs are **cloned** in a clever way. The scientist finds a blood-sucking insect from dinosaur times. It became trapped in a substance called amber. The amber kept the insect in fresh condition. The insect had sucked the blood of dinosaurs. These blood **cells** were still within the insect's body. The scientist uses the **DNA** from these blood cells to clone the dinosaurs.

But scientists say this is very unlikely. The insect would have to have been trapped in amber almost immediately after biting a dinosaur. Even then, the dinosaur blood would not have stayed fresh enough to preserve its cells.

The dodo became extinct in the late 1600s. If it could be brought back by cloning, do you think it could survive?

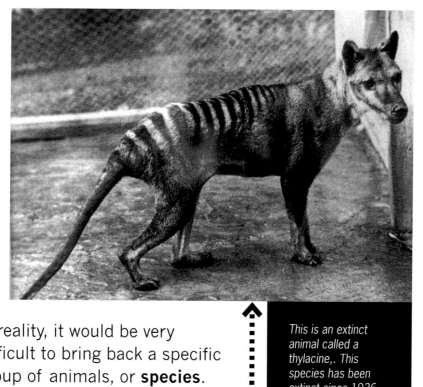

In reality, it would be very difficult to bring back a specific group of animals, or **species**. Scientists would need a lot of the animals' cells. That is because cloning takes many tries to work.

This is an extinct animal called a thylacine,. This species has been extinct since 1936.

Also, an animal must serve as a **surrogate** mother. So far, all surrogates have been similar to the clones. For instance, another sheep gave birth to Dolly. There are some **extinct** animals with close relatives that are still alive. For example, an elephant might be able to give birth to an extinct woolly mammoth. But could any animal give birth to a cloned dinosaur?

Even if scientists could clone a lot of an extinct species, where would we put them? When an animal dies out, other animals take its place in nature. Would adding a species of clones disturb this balance? Also, the cloned animals would be born in enclosed areas. How would they learn to survive in the wild?

Can cloning help save endangered species?

In 2000 scientists **cloned** a gaur. This is a rare type of ox from India. This was the first time an **endangered species** had been cloned. (*Endangered* means in danger of dying out.) Since then, scientists have cloned several different endangered species. They include types of wild sheep, cattle, and wildcats.

But could all this really help endangered species survive? The answer is not clear yet. Some organizations have stored samples of wild animal **DNA** for many years. Around the world there may be over a million samples representing at least 700 different species. Cloning endangered animals might help keep up their numbers.

These animals are a kind of endangered Asian cow called the Javan banteng. Thanks to cloning, they still exist.

WORD STORE   endangered in danger of dying out

These white rhinos in South Africa are endangered. Should humans try everything, even cloning, to help them?

But endangered species face many dangers. Human activity is destroying wildlife where animals live. Pollution (dirty air and water), overhunting, and other threats could wipe out many species. Unless these issues are dealt with, endangered species will remain in serious danger.

Many environmental groups are afraid that people will see cloning as an easy answer to a much larger problem. They point out that saving endangered species is difficult work. They believe that people should focus on fixing problems like pollution instead.

Even so, many scientists agree that cloning can help species "buy time" until conditions improve.

PET CLONING AND PUBLIC OPINION

Pet cloning remains very unpopular with the public. For instance, in May 2004 some Americans were asked what they thought of pet cloning. About 64 percent of them disapproved of pet cloning. Only 32 percent approved. These people said they supported animal cloning only for research purposes. Most of them opposed cloning just to re-create a pet.

Will we all own cloned pets one day?

It seems unlikely that one day we will all own **cloned** pets. This is mostly because pet cloning is expensive.

Sir Lancelot Encore cost his owners about $155,000. Scientists have learned cost-saving measures since then. But cloned pets remain very expensive. Today, the price of cloned dogs is about $50,000. A cloned cat might cost around $32,000.

The costs of cloning pets will likely continue to drop over time. Scientists will become better and faster at cloning processes. They will find ways to make it cheaper. This is especially true if the demand for cloning pets increases. More and more cloning companies will compete for business. They will have to drop their prices to attract customers.

But cloning remains a highly complex procedure. Only a few skilled scientists can do it. That means pet cloning will likely remain something only wealthy people can afford.

But even if it is affordable, pet cloning is not something everyone wants to do. (See the box at left.) Some people might choose to clone a pet. But other people will probably choose to start a new relationship with a new pet.

PET CLONING TIMELINE

1673 Dutch scientist Anton van Leeuwenhoek becomes the first person to see living **cells**. He uses a simple microscope that he made himself.

1831 Scottish scientist Robert Brown shows that the **nucleus** is the most important part of the cell.

1839 German scientists Theodor Schwann and Mathias Schleiden create the "cell theory of life." It states that all life is made up of cells.

1860s Austrian monk Gregor Mendel studies pea plants. He wants to find out how **genes** pass on things like flower color and seed shape. His work is ignored until the early 1900s.

1952 U.S. scientists Robert Briggs and Thomas J. King **clone** northern leopard frogs. They use the cells of **embryos**. These are the first animals to be cloned by scientists.

1953 U.S. scientist James Watson and English scientist Francis Crick show the structure of **DNA**. This discovery paves the way for many other breakthroughs in the study of genes.

1953–1960s Further experiments with frogs improve scientists' knowledge about cloning.

1963 English scientist J. B. S. Haldane coins the word *clone*.

1969 U.S. scientists James Shapiro and Jonathan Beckwith identify the first gene.

1977 Scientists clone mice using the cells of embryos.

1984 Danish scientist Steen Willadsen uses embryo cells to clone sheep. Within two years, other scientists use embryo cells to clone a cow.

1996 Scottish scientists Ian Wilmut and Keith Campbell create Dolly. She is the first clone of a **mammal** using adult cells instead of embryo cells. In the next decade, researchers will clone many farm animals.

1997 The creation of Dolly sparks fears that human **reproductive cloning** will happen soon. In Europe, this process of creating an animal with identical DNA to another is not allowed to be used on humans. The U.S. government cuts off all funding for human cloning.

2001 CC, or Copy Cat, becomes the first pet ever cloned. That same year researchers produce a gaur (a type of ox). It is the first cloned **endangered species**.

2003 Researchers clone Ditteaux, a rare type of African wildcat.

2004 South Korean scientist Hwang Woo-suk claims that he has cloned a human embryo. His claims later turn out to be false.

2005 Snuppy, the first cloned dog, is born in South Korea.

GLOSSARY

artificial something made by humans, rather than by nature

breed control how animals mate and reproduce

cell tiny building block of life

clone copy of a plant or animal that shares the same genetic makeup as the original. The word is also used to describe the act of making the copy.

deoxyrybonucleic acid (DNA) substance within a cell's nucleus. It carries genes, the instructions for how a body is made up.

diversity variety

embryo animal in an early step of growth

endangered in danger of dying out

extinct died out

gene stretch of DNA that carries instructions for life. It is found within cells.

gene cloning scientific process in which cloning is used to reproduce copies of genes or segments of DNA. Gene cloning is widely used to study genes that pass on diseases within families.

genetic relating to genes

genetic engineering process in which scientists change the genes within the DNA coding of a plant or animal

immune system body system that helps fight disease

mammal animal that gives milk to its young and usually has hair or fur

myth idea not based on fact

nucleus control center of a cell. It contains the cell's DNA, or instructions for how a body is made up.

offspring young (babies)

primate group of animals that includes monkeys, apes, and humans

reproduce make young (babies) or copies

reproductive cloning scientific process that creates an animal with the same DNA, or instructions for how a body is made up, as another animal. Dolly the sheep and Encore the dog were created through reproductive cloning.

species group of similar animals that is created in nature

stem cell special kind of cell taken from an egg. Stem cells can be used to create any type of cell in the human body.

surrogate substitute. A clone is inserted into a surrogate mother, which gives birth to the clone.

telomere part of DNA that is like an internal clock for a cell

therapeutic cloning scientific process in which human embryos are cloned for research. They create stem cells. Researchers hope that stem cells can be used as replacement cells to treat certain diseases.

FIND OUT MORE

BOOKS

Balkwill, Frances R., and Mic Rolph. *Gene Machines*. Cold Spring Harbor, N.Y.: Cold Spring Harbor Laboratory Press, 2002.

Cefrey, Holly. *Cloning and Genetic Engineering*. Danbury, Conn.: Children's Press, 2002.

Cohen, Daniel. *Cloning*. Brookfield, Conn.: Twenty-First Century, 2002.

Walker, Richard. *Genes & DNA*. Boston: Kingfisher, 2007.

WEBSITES

ASPCA Position Statement on Pet Cloning
www.aspca.org/about-us/policy-positions/pet-cloning. html
Read the viewpoint of the ASPCA (American Society for the Prevention of Cruelty to Animals) on pet cloning.

Cloning: The Real Truth
http://library.thinkquest.org/J002564F/Cloning%20 Website.htm
Find more information on cloning and its history at this website. You can also take a quiz and participate in a poll on human cloning.

On Human Cloning: Three Views
http://www.pbs.org/wgbh/nova/baby/cloning.html
This PBS website presents three different arguments about cloning.

TOPICS TO LEARN MORE ABOUT

- **Genetically modified (GM) foods**
  In this book, you have learned that some foods are cloned. Research other forms of genetic engineering in the food industry. What are the benefits according to supporters? What kinds of problems do critics see?

- **Saving endangered animals**
  As you have seen, there have been attempts to use cloning to save endangered animal species. But some critics argue that this is not the best option. Do further research on this issue to find out what the experts think. What arguments are made in favor of cloning endangered animals? What arguments are made against it?

INDEX